HOLIDAYING

50 YEARS OF ADVERTISING & PUBLICITY RELATING TO HOLIDAYS

RUTH ARTMONSKY & STELLA HARPLEY

Published by:
Artmonsky Arts
Flat 1, 27 Henrietta Street
London WC2E 8NA
artmonskyruth@gmail.com
Tel. 020 7240 8774

Text © Ruth Artmonsky 2019

ISBN 978-0-9935878-7-0

Designed by:
David Preston Studio
www.davidprestonstudio.com

Printed in England by:
Northend Creative Print Solutions
www.northend.co.uk

As usual, my thanks go to my designers David and Tamsin at David Preston Studio for their innovation and wit.

CONTENTS

FOREWORD

Although I was born in London, I'd like to be considered at least an 'honorary,' if not a full, 'sand-grown'un'. My grandmother ran a kosher theatrical boarding house in Southend; her cousin, Younkman toured the piers and resort theatres with his Czardas Band; I was brought up in Thorpe Bay and Blackpool; and over the years have holidayed regularly in Aldeburgh and Brighton. At various times, the family has had holiday homes at Brighton and St. Ives, and we haven't been slouches when it comes to holidays abroad – I, with all my equipment on my back, nudist camping in the south of France to later sejours at the Negresco. The Danielli and the Mamounia; Stella was an undergraduate in Brighton, and has been altogether more adventurous, catamaran sailing in the Seychelles, walking the philosopher's path in Japan, and riding a camel called Michael Jackson on the Pakistani border.

But can we therefore be considered experts on holidays, on what attracts people to take breaks from their everyday life, just because we've taken a multitude of such breaks ourselves? When writing a book on the interior design of liners I came across a Lady Brocklebank, wife of a Cunard chairman, who considered that because she was much travelled on the company's ships she was well-qualified to take over the interior design of a new one! So the answer to my question as to our expertise is definitely 'No'! But we do know something about advertising and that has given us the excuse to plug into our nostalgia and enthusiasm for holidaying and holiday resorts, to compile this book.

'A basic and most desirable human activity, deserving the praise and encouragement of all peoples and all Governments.'

The United Nations on tourism, 1967

INTRODUCTION

How the idea of having a 'holiday' began is given in the word itself 'holi-day' – days that were determined by the church as having a particularly sacred significance. These came to be celebrated with ceremonies and festivities, often specific to a local area. Overtime the 'sacredness' of the day dwindled and the festivities increased so the days became more secular, more like holidays than days of worship and ritual. Traces of the sanctity aspect remained when workers chose to extend their break from the weekend to the Monday, it became coloquially known as St. Monday! The Bank Holiday Act of 1870, and its extension of 1875 confirmed the traditional 'holy' days as Easter, Whitsun and Christmas and added Boxing Day and the first Monday in August.

But the idea that workers should have, by right, further days off work, and that such time should be paid for by their employer, was very slow in being accepted, even by the workers themselves. Where people were employed in large factories, as in the cotton mills of

Lancashire, they were able to gain informal arrangements for time off without pay and such time morphed into 'wakes weeks' where whole factories, and sometimes towns, would down tools, and for those who could afford it, holiday at the seaside. Savings or 'going off' clubs were started not only at works, but sometimes at a local pub or for a whole street, so that people could cover the likely costs of such breaks. Such arrangements were fewer in the south of England, where work tended to be organised in small workshops and workers consequently lacked the power to make deals.

It was not really until the emergence of trade unions and the formation of the Labour party in the early years of the twentieth century, and until these bodies took any sort of interest in the 'time off work' issue, that national legislation was brought in. Well ahead of this, by 1920, some of the 'white collar' unions, such as those for the Civil Service and local government, had, by sheer force of numbers, achieved two weeks paid leave; whilst cotton mill workers, through their unions, had agreed annual holidays of one hundred and sixteen and a half hours, (just under five days), as early as 1906. The legislation, when it did come, with the Holidays with Pay Act of 1938, was a weak compromise, did not cover all workers, and was, in fact, delayed by the onset of war. Susan Barton, in her study of working class tourism, surprisingly asserted that until this Act the majority of workers could not even contemplate a week's holiday and provides the statistic that until the Act only one third of workers took holidays away from home at all. Nevertheless, by 1960, some twenty-seven

Above: Advertisement from the *Tatler* for Revelation luggage, 'The World's Most Famous Suitcase', 1937.

Left: An early travel poster for Thos. Cook & Son, undated.

Opposite page: Bookmark publicising the Royal Mail Steam Packet Company, 1921.

million workers, either by legislation or by voluntary agreements had paid holiday provision.

Meanwhile, at the other end of the social spectrum, the few, aristocratic and wealthy, who had taken Grand Tours on the Continent in the eighteenth century, ostensibly for educational purposes but largely for pleasure, had been replaced by larger numbers holidaying at spas and watering holes. The declared purpose of such visits was for improving their health, but alongside this much pleasure was derived from the socializing and entertaining laid on. And once King George III had dipped his toe in the sea at Weymouth in the 1780s, again because of possible health benefits. there followed a cascading that converted small villages and fishing harbours around the British coast into seaside resorts. Similarly, when the British discovered the south of France, it was not for summer holidays but for improved health in the winter – the 'fashionable' season did not shift to the summer months and from therapy to pleasure, until well into the twentieth century. Nevertheless, British holiday resorts continued to make much of the health-giving qualities of their respective boroughs in their advertising and publicity, detailing such matters as degrees of sunshine, cleanliness of tap water and control of sewage. And throughout the inter-war years the benefits of being out in the open air and being active were advocated by such voluntary bodies as the Youth Hostelling Association, the Ramblers Association and even the Labour Party in its campaigns for better recreational facilities; all encouraging people to use their free time for recharging, as well as for entertainment.

STAGGERED HOLIDAYS FOR COMFORT

there's more room, remember, in June and September

HINTS FOR A HAPPY HOLIDAY

We have prepared this leaflet to help you overcome some of the little problems that may occur. It's well worth reading carefully, and taking with you—especially if you've not travelled abroad before.

Poster encouraging holiday-makers to stagger their holidays, design by Eileen Evans, undated.

Pamphlet offering 'Hints for a Happy Holiday' for those travelling abroad, undated.

Of course, holidays for the masses would not have been possible but for developments in transport albeit communities were wont to walk or horse ride to the sea, before the arrival of the railways. From the mid-nineteenth century onwards, trains made it practical for large numbers to be conveyed long distances, quickly and relatively cheaply. Railway networks spread their tentacles towards the coast and a symbiotic relationship grew up between the resorts and the railway companies – resorts needed visitors and railways needed passengers – they fed each other.

Once the combustion engine had been invented, the charabanc, an early bus, and then the coach, provided an even cheaper means for people to go on holidays, both for getting to their destinations and for touring. For the better off, once ships had morphed from sail to steam, from hazardous to reliable, cruising became a possibility. And then again, after WWII, with redundant aircraft and unemployed pilots, young opportunistic entrepreneurs launched the air borne 'package'. By the mid-1960s five million Britishers were holidaying abroad, and 30 million at home – mass holiday migration became the norm.

Yet class differences remained – stations had first class waiting, rooms and trains first class carriages – and later, with air travel those going abroad tended to be younger and better off, those staying within British boundaries, older and poorer. And when it came to destinations, the middle classes tended to holiday in the quiet of the Lake District or at the less developed parts of the coasts of East Anglia, Cornwall and Devon, the working class heading for the noise

Above: Souvenir Programme for Dover, 'East Kent Record Sunshine', undated.

Opposite page, left: Leaflet publicising Worthing, 'For Sunshine Music & Flowers', undated.

Opposite page, right: Leaflet publicising Bridlington, undated.

and bustle of Blackpool, Southend, and the like. And with holidays abroad the middle class retained the Riviera as their province, the masses adopting Spain, Greece and Yugoslavia.

But although more and more people were eager, and increasingly able, to take holidays, the providers of such, the resorts, the agents, the servicers, needed to have a constant flow of customers for economic viability; competition became fierce, sometimes cut-throat. The rapidly developing professions of advertising and public relations were increasingly called upon to arm the combatants. And again, the railways were ahead of the game, LNER the leader and Southern trailing behind, LNER signing up some of the most talented commercial artists of the time. Advertising and publicity, in the form of posters, leaflets and brochures became crucial; resorts competed with each other as to which was the healthiest and which offered the better entertainments; and with the 'air' packages, which was the quickest, the cheapest and the one providing most comforts and exotic views.

Because the railway posters, often the result of collaboration between resorts and railway companies, have been so comprehensively covered already in the splendidly illustrated volumes produced under licence from the National Museum of Science and Industry, in this book we are concentrating on lesser known holiday advertising and publicity, together with lesser known artists. The form of this publicity extends beyond the poster, to include: brochures, leaflets and press advertisements.

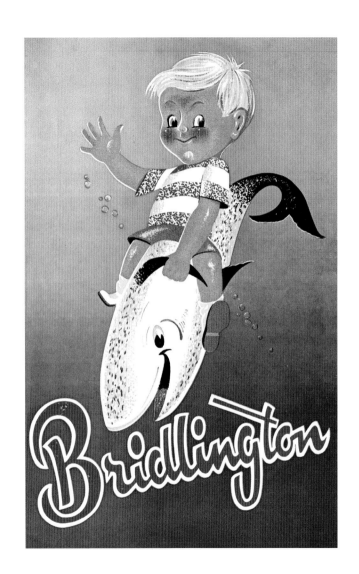

PACKING

Although social historians of holidays have shown some interest in events preceding a holiday, as to how working-class people managed to put together enough money to go on holiday, and how much depended on the development of transport systems for getting to holiday destinations, very few have given more than a glance at anticipation – the imagining of what was to come and how to pack to cover all eventualities.

Thomas Cook, from the start, advised holidaymakers to 'travel light', with 'the jaunty swagger of unencumbered bachelorhood', albeit for his early Continental trips he suggested they packed 'soap and tea'. And when he opened his travel shop in London, in the 1860s, he sold, amongst other things, guide books, maps, bags, waterproof knapsacks, hat cases, telescopes and Alpine footwear, all of which would have very much 'cumbered' his clients on their travels and could hardly have fitted into his recommended carpet bag. Even in its post-WWII 'Hints for your holidays' Cook's still maintained 'travel light' –

> A medium-sized suitcase should hold everything you need
> on holiday and its weight would normally be within the free
> baggage allowance.

At the other end of the baggage continuum were the cruise companies who implied anything goes when it came to packing for a cruise. A 1933 Orient Line pamphlet declared –

18

Cook's brochure on preparing for one's holiday, undated.

There is practically no limit to the amount of baggage that may be taken.

And in the same year P&O offering cruises to the West Indies advertised similarly –

The quantity of baggage which is stored in commodious baggage rooms, always accessible, is practically without limit.

The first holidaymakers abroad after the end of WWII, with great scarcity across Europe, were, in fact, encouraged to take with them everything they might need, as many of them would have done anyway, suspecting that none of what they considered essential would culturally be known to 'foreigners'. Against such overloading were the air package companies and touring coach companies, who, like Cook, advised economy. Lunn's tours in 1950 made this a virtue – 'To save trouble and expense take as little luggage as possible.'

Both technical developments in the material sciences and transport systems were to have a major influence on the design of what luggage holidaymakers used. Obviously if one had been journeying on a stagecoach or in a sailing ship what was required was solidity and weather resistance, and early trunks tended to be made of wood, sometimes of leather and waterproofed with canvas. When car ownership grew, in the 1930s and luggage was frequently strapped outside, strength and weatherproofing were still all important.

Efficient Luggage for Easter Jaunts

BOLSTER BAG (on left)

Light, capacious and conveniently fitted with 'lightning' fastener. In good quality grained hide, leather lined.

Size 18 ins. 55/-   20 ins. 60/-   22 ins. 65/-
Size 24 ins. 70/-   26 ins. 75/-   28 ins. 81/-

Trunks, First Floor

MOTOR TRUNK (on right)

A practical trunk of new design, with domed top, strongly made of three-ply, lined and covered with Rexine. Water-tight and dust-proof, it contains two full-size black suit cases and is fitted with lever clips and dust-proof locks.

30 × 17½ × 16 ins. £7 7 0
33 × 17½ × 16 ins. £8 2 6
36 × 17½ × 16 ins. £8 15 0

Three-ply Trunk, covered in strong leather-cloth, with fibre binding.
30 × 17½ × 16 ins. . · . . . £5 5 0

HARRODS LTD   **HARRODS**   LONDON SW1

Above right: Advertisement for Harrod's 'motor trunk' designed for road towing, 1929.

Harrods advertised a motor trunk in 1929 as 'strongly built of three-ply, lined and covered in Rexine.'

But it was air travel that was to have the most dramatic influence on the design of holiday luggage – certainly with restrictions as to weight and dimensions. Fairways Continental Coach Tours, in the 1950s, advised their customers who were travelling by air, to take only one suitcase, weighing 30lbs with the dimensions 30x15x9 inches. And then, perhaps a more indirect influence, with the burgeoning size of airports entailing increased walking with luggage, came the addition of wheels to luggage. Initially on a separate band strapped to the case, but then integral to the case's construction. Although there had been wheeled trunks advertised as early as the

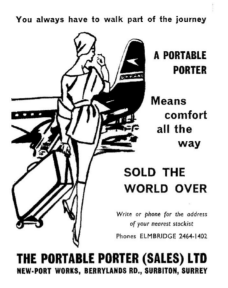

You always have to walk part of the journey

A PORTABLE PORTER

Means comfort all the way

SOLD THE WORLD OVER

Write or phone for the address of your nearest stockist

Phones ELMBRIDGE 2464-1402

THE PORTABLE PORTER (SALES) LTD
NEW-PORT WORKS, BERRYLANDS RD., SURBITON, SURREY

WITH YOUR "LEAVE" MA'AM

THE qualities of good judgment which have raised these well-trained, well-disciplined women to commissioned rank, are certain to have guided their preference for Antler Travel Goods—the lightest, sturdiest and smartest-looking cases ever made—in the days before these became—like appreciations of good service—few and far between.

ANTLER
The Aristocrat of TRAVEL GOODS

Manufactured by
J. B. BROOKS & CO. LTD., BIRMINGHAM.
THE WORLD'S BEST LUGGAGE

Above right: Post-war advertisement for wheeled luggage, undated.

Above far right: Antler wartime advertisement, 1942.

1880s, surprisingly wheels did not become a standard feature until after WWII.

When it came to materials, wood and, most often for working class holiday makers, cardboard, would eventually give way to fiberglass and aluminium; metal locks to zips, and brown or neutral finishes to colour, and sometimes pattern. An advertisement for Airstream, in 1960, offered cases in smoke blue, Burma red and ivory.

Luggage, like other acoutrement, was used to show off. Whereas for early holiday makers the wealthy could seem carefree in the number of trunks and cases they travelled with, servants, railway porters and hotel bellboys being at hand, the lower classes had largely to carry their luggage themselves. Even when the porters etc.

began to disappear and luggage got lighter, the wealth of holiday makers could immediately be discerned by the 'style' of their cases, and, indeed, if they had more than one they would be matching. A Tatler advertisement in 1933 advertised a travel dressing case with nine carat gold fittings, and Louis Vuitton was to shout class with its brand-patterned surfaces. Luggage became a fashion statement and even lesser brands more frequently advertised in the British press, as Antler and Revelation, were also to hype their products as not mere containers but as 'of the moment'. Revelation, advertising in *The Queen* in 1960 advised –

This year holiday in style with the most glamorous luggage you could ever wish to see.

Antler, too, although offering marginally less expensive luggage, advertised itself as –

…the aristocrat of travel goods.

Having decided what to pack one's essentials in, given that one had options which the majority did not, the next decision was what these essentials should be; the bulk proved to be clothes.

What people wore on holiday obviously would depend on means, and to a lesser extent on fashion. 'Best clothes' which were what one wore on Sundays or for special celebrations, was what working class holiday makers wore, not only to travel in, but for walking along the promenade and on the beach. A Mass Observation survey of 1938 described the promenade as 'the scene's a parade of all in 'Sunday Best' in honour of the occasion.' Through until WWII, men would

Antler advert marking the arrival
of coloured luggage sets, 1965.

Revelation advert playing on Breakfast
at Tiffany's Holly Golightly, undated.

ANY BATHING SUIT WON'T DO

It will be hard to decide between the apple-green and black with the orange belt, and that heavenly kingfisher blue bound with white. But when you've seen the tempting colours and the thrilling designs, when you've felt the soft, springy wool, and noticed the firm knit and trim tailoring and the low price—you'll know that this year it must be a Wolsey bathing suit.

Think how you'll look in one on the shore, when the sun brings out your colour and you get nice and brown. Picture yourself lazing on the sand, riding a ninth wave on one of those preposterous sea-horses.

Any of these suits will fit you to perfection, only the colour has to be decided. And the fit will be neat and natty all the season, the suit won't shrink or sag or lose shape.

All the colours are sea-fast. And Wolsey bathing suits give employment to British people in Leicester—which in these times is worth remembering.

WOLSEY BATHING SUITS

be found sitting in deck chairs in suits, ofttimes with a cap on their heads; women travelled with hats and gloves, but possibly were rather more brazen when on the beach. Susan Barton records their having rubber knickers to wear over their skirts to prevent them getting wet when paddling; and old holiday photographs show women tucking their flowery frocks into elasticated bloomers. Akhtar & Humphries concluded that –

> Most men, like T.S. Eliot's Prufrock, considered that rolling up their trousers and perhaps loosening their tie or exchanging flat caps for knotted handkerchiefs as they paddled along the shore,

Opposite page, left: Advertisement for Wolsey bathing suits, from *Punch*, 1930.

Opposite page, right: Jantzen advertisement, from *Punch*, 1939.

Right: Martha Harris Autumn window display for Jaeger Sea Wear, 1933.

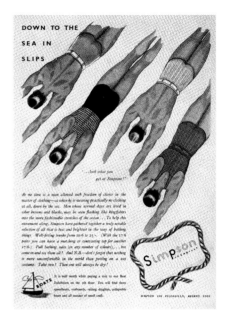

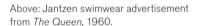

Above: Jantzen swimwear advertisement from *The Queen*, 1960.

Above right: Jantzen swimwear advertisement from *The Queen*, 1960.

Above far right: Simpson's swimwear advert, illustrated by Hof (Max Hoff), undated.

to be quite daring enough.

Sometimes the travel agent or tour operator would offer advice as to what clothes to pack. Cook's always stressed the need for sensible footwear if much walking was to be involved, particularly for its Continental packages – 'boots with good firm soles'. And most agents, for sun-seeking holidays nevertheless suggested a mac or waterproof as the sun didn't necessarily shine all the time.

Obviously, those camping or caravanning were advised entirely differently from those cruising! An inter-war AA brochure for campers suggested khaki shirts (as washing facilities were limited), overalls (for work on the car when it broke down), Wellingtons (for muddy camp sites), and several pairs of socks (for chilly nights); but did add 'best clothes' (which should be packed in separate suitcases). Over the same years the cruise lines, in their brochure texts and illustrations, implied that evening clothes were essential for dining and dancing. But even for cruising there were hints that all might not be fair weather. P&O in its advertising of winter cruises to the West Indies and South America in 1933 advised –

> Some warm clothing and underwear should be taken as well as summer clothing; also a rug, rubber-soled deck shoes and walking boots for use ashore.

In the early post-WWII years much was made of the different customs abroad when it came to clothes. This was particularly so in the years when there was currency control and suitable clothing might have to be purchased quickly so as not to offend locals. This applied especially for visits to churches – neither sex should wear shorts, and women were advised not to wear slacks (trousers) and to see they had covering for their heads and arms. Many tour operators would also point out appropriate clothes to be worn in hotels, both during the day and in the evening. Cook's, warning their clients that beach clothes should not be worn for dining added –

> For the evening meal it is usual to dress up a little... men usually wear a dark suit and a tie.

But by the 1930s clothes were getting lighter and briefer, and consequently taking up less room in the luggage; none more so than the bathing costume. In the early years of the twentieth century women would dip in the sea in voluminous garb, made heavy by the

materials used, and weighted down at the hem so that they shouldn't rise in the water. Modesty was all important – no hint should be given of the shape of the body within. Even men (who had largely bathed nude before this was banned in the 1860s), besported costumes that resembled long underwear.

The key to the radical change was the substitute of the word 'swim' for that of 'bathing'. The beach and the sea that had previously been visited for health, in the 20s and 30s became places for sunning and sporting. A Jantzen advertisement in *Punch* in the 1930s hyped the 'speed-suit' –

> …trunks, neck and armhole are cut to the minimum, freedom for a powerful stroke.

Comfort of movement and briefness for sunbathing were points now made in swimwear advertising – arms of costumes had disappeared, legs were shortened to the thigh, and the neck dropped; men's costumes lost their tops (a fashion previously only allowed on Brighton beaches).

Typical advertising of swimwear was that of Wolsey, one of the leading British swimwear manufacturers of the 1930s –

> …of smooth soft wool with an elastic close-ribbed knit that makes them fit, in the water and out of it, just like an extra skin.

Meridian, a competitor in the swimwear business, in a 1930 *Punch* advertisement was also stressing 'the perfect fit' –

> What's the point of a bathing costume that rumples and crumples and slips off your shoulders, or else grips so inflexibly

Beach and holiday clothes, 1957.

Above: Spread from a brochure for Simpson of Picadilly, undated.

Above right: Advertisement for Simpson's beach and holiday clothes, 1957.

Opposite page: Tampax advertisement, from *Home & Gardens,* 1949.

that it chafes you at every movement?'
And then, in the 1940s came the bikini. Two-piece swimwear for women had been marketed before the war but had usually consisted of shorts and a top often with short sleeves. Initially banned in Spain, Portugal and Italy, the bikini eventually became the most popular form of swimwear for women.

The advertising of holiday clothes was seasonal – from Easter through to July – with most of the large stores in London and beyond building extravagant displays of liner decks, tropical islands, and the like, to display the fashions of the moment. Some retailers actually linked up with travel firms, each scratching the other's back, such as

Travel sick ? Never ! WE TAKE KWELLS

Make sure travel-sickness doesn't spoil your family journey. Simply take Kwells. Kwells contain hyoscine, *safely used as a medicine through the ages*, and proved by independent medical tests in the last few years to be the most effective travel-sickness preventive.

Proved too by hundreds of thousands of families by road, rail, sea and air.

Take Kwells, the proven *safe* travel-sickness remedy, before you start your journey.

FROM YOUR CHEMIST 2/3d.

1950s advertisement for popular travel sickness remedy Kwells.

You need the protection of POND'S

During your holiday more than at any other time you need *Pond's Vanishing Cream.* It protects from sunburn and the harshening effects of sea water, gives the skin a beautiful bloom, and makes a lasting and reliable base for your powder. Used in conjunction with *Pond's Cold Cream, Pond's Cleansing Tissues,* and *Pond's Skin Freshener,* it keeps the skin fine and smooth and the complexion beautifully clear. If you are not already a user of these preparations, send 1/- to Pond's Extract Co., (Dept. 504,) 103, St. John St., London, E.C.1, who will send you a four-sample package to try.

OBTAINABLE FROM CHEMISTS, STORES & HIGH CLASS HAIRDRESSERS.

Pond's Vanishing Cream, **Opal Jars, 2/6 and 1/3. Tubes 1/- and 6d.**
Pond's Cold Cream, **Opal Jars, 5/-, 2/6 and 1/3. Tubes, 2/6, 1/- and 6d.**
Pond's Cleansing Tissues, **per box, 2/-, 1/3, & 9d.**
Pond's Skin Freshener, **per bottle, 5/6, 3/- & 1/-**

Pond's
COLD CREAM,
CLEANSING TISSUES,
SKIN FRESHENER,
VANISHING CREAM.

Pond's advertisement, from *Home Chat*, 1929.

In case you need it on holiday

Change of diet—change of air—change of routine . . . all these can upset your stomach and spoil your holiday. To make sure you have a wonderful time, keep MEGGESON Bismuth Dyspepsia Tablets handy, and enjoy quick relief from indigestion at all times. Pocket tin 1/8. Home-use bottle 4/3½. Obtainable from chemists only.

Meggeson BISMUTH DYSPEPSIA TABLETS

Advertisement for Meggeson tablets, a popular upset tummy remedy, from *Men's Only*, 1955.

Swan & Edgar at Piccadilly cooperating with the Royal Mail Line for the display of cruise wear. Crawford's was the advertising agency used by both Simpson's and Jaeger for their summer clothes brochures and press advertisements, the former frequently illustrated by Hof (Max Hoff). Jaeger, from the late 1930s was to use Colman, Prentis & Varley (an offspring of Crawford's) and created some stir with its swimwear windows designed by Martha Harris with not a tailor's dummy in sight, the costumes displayed flat.

Although it was health concerns that contributed so much to the early growth of holiday destinations, whether in the countryside or at the seaside, there have been remarkably few commentators of possible unhealthy moments, and the need to pack to deal with them – children spewing out of car windows, everyone spewing on boat decks or on early flights, tummy 'bugs' with foreign food, raw skin from over-enthusiastic sunbathing, or just how women coped with periods with not a pharmacy in sight. The well-prepared suitcase packer would have calculated a space for all the creams, lotions and pills that should be taken 'just in case'.

For sickness, whether on the road, at sea, or in a plane, Kwells seems to have been the most popular solution, with its magic ingredient of hyoscine, the specific formula having evolved from wartime experimentation for troops on the move. Early Kwell's advertisements in the late 1940s would play on this carrying such tags as 'The D-Day remedy'. An early post-war leaflet put out by CIT mentions 'some ships are fitted with stabilisers' and 'some airlines now fly above the weather line' suggesting that most were not and did not.

Rennies was the answer for tummy troubles, and Aspro for headaches. But the AA's advice to campers and caravanners suggested a range of other ailments to be prepared for 'cuts, burns, stings, mosquito bites and sunburn'; and added the need for brandy or rum 'for emergencies and warding off a chill'.

But it was the possible effect of the sun and the weather that perhaps attracted the largest and certainly the most colourful press advertising for the health of the holidaymaker. Victorians and Edwardian, desiring to look pale, were advised by the likes of the Baedeker Guides to pack hats, veils and gloves. Exposing the skin to wind and water was said to have its dangers, and people, into the 1920s and 30s, by then preferring a tanned look, were faced with a fine balance between desiring to get brown yet not get burnt, to look bronzed but not wrinkled; any link with cancer was unknown at the time. Pond's, whose products could be purchased at Woolworths, was early on the scene targeting holidaymakers, as with a 1929 advertisement in *Home Chat* –

> During your holidays more than at any other time you need Pond's Vanishing Cream. It protects from sunburn and the hardening effects of sea water.

At the other end of the market both Helena Rubenstein and Elizabeth Arden were developing 'sun' products, Elizabeth Arden claiming that with hers –

> Neither wind nor sunrays will alter the purity and brilliance of your complexion.

Like Pond's, Nivea had been selling a general skin care cream but began to appreciate the problems and popularity of tanning so started marketing it, along with a sun oil, as serving both purposes: healthy skin and bronzing. A 1939 *Home Notes* advertisement hyped –

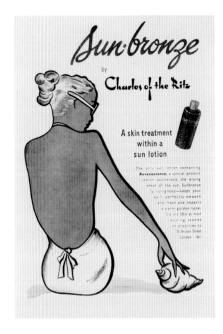

Above: Advertisement for Charles of the Ritz sun lotion, from *The Queen*, 1953.

Right: Nivea advertisement from *John Bull* magazine, 1954.

BINOCULARS
and your
Holidays.

NOTHING will add so much to the delights of your holidays as a pair of Ross Binoculars.

There will be hundreds of occasions when you will long to get a nearer view of some distant landscape, a far off mountain, or passing shipping.

Every day a pair of Ross glasses will add to the interest and pleasure of the holiday. Things you have never seen before will readily come to your vision and incidents which would have otherwise passed unnoticed will reveal their story to amuse and entertain you.

Send for a copy of our illustrated booklet on the use of Binoculars. Sent post free on request.

Get a pair of Ross Binoculars before completing your holiday arrangements, but be sure they bear the name of "Ross." These alone will give you that brilliant definition and fineness of detail which is so essential.

ROSS LTD

Clapham Common, S.W.4.
West End Showrooms,
13/14, Great Castle Street,
Oxford Circus, W.1.
And at 100, Deansgate, Manchester.

Above: 1930s advertisement for Ross Binoculars.

Right: Advertisement for Polaroid sunglasses, from *Vogue*, 1953.

Only Nivea contains Eucerite an ingredient chiefly responsible for skin protection and for obtaining that much desired natural and healthy sun bronzed appearance.

Miriam Akhtar and Steve Humphries write amusingly of the craze for getting brown –

Tans were planned like military operations and whole days and weeks would be spent on holiday nurturing the right shade of brown to come home with. A tanned look seemed to denote status, sex, money, sophistication and good health and it was a look most people of all ages wanted.

The product that most conjured up the image of 'sex, money and sophistication' was Ambre Solaire, launched by L'Oreal in 1935 as helping people to 'tan naturally without burning'.

The mania for tanning not only brought a whole lot of new skin products to the market but came to make sun-glasses not only an essential to be packed but a fashion statement. Cook's began to recommend the inclusion of sun glasses in one's packing as did Sky Tours and other package tour agents. Polaroid had been founded just prior to the onset of war and soon became the market leader, having improved the technical qualities of its glasses by wartime work for aviators. Its glasses claimed to make eyes 'cool and comfortable, even in the strongest sun glare.'

Unlike ordinary sun glasses which darken everything you see, Polaroid sunglasses, with their selective control over light, enable you to see through reflected glare yet retain clear detail and sparkling colour in everything you would wish to see. Ideal for Holidays.

Yet another essential to pack was the Box Brownie. Few texts on the history of holidays are without sepia photos of happy families building sandcastles or wearing silly hats and the like; and how many attics are piled high with boxes of photograph albums, occasionally brought out for family get-togethers. Susan Barton acutely observed that '...in the creation of memory photography is a vitally important factor', and much of adults' memories of childhood are likely to have been reconstructed from holiday photos of the time. Although, perhaps, along the Riviera, the odd Leica would have been sported, for the majority of British holidaymakers in the interwar years the Brownie was what was invariably packed. Kodak's Brownie was marketed from the turn of the century and was sold cheaply, as the company was to make its money selling the rolls of films and processing paper that were part and parcel of the photographic process. It was the Brownie that sold the idea of the snapshot to the masses; and one of the most iconic seaside photographs, Bert Hardy's image, of two girls sitting on railings at Blackpool, is said to have been taken with one. By the 1920s Kodak was advertising extensively in the British press. A *Punch* advertisement of 1928 conjured up –

Kodak Holiday Magazine, 1937.

> ...in the winter evening they'll be enjoying their holiday stills.
> Such a small item in the luggage – a little black box.

The name Kodak was to be seen everywhere, on the high street, at Butlin's holiday camps, even Cook's urged its clients to – 'Take a Kodak camera and bring back the fun!'

For those holidaying abroad some agents advised taking Continental electric plugs, whilst others thought them readily available abroad. And many advised the odd phrase book, with Linguaphone

Click! went the 'Kodak'

Great fun—a 'Kodak,' and yet it is fun that yields abiding fruit.
It makes in half a second a thing which may last half a century.
"Click" is all it says, and yet it speaks volumes. Get your own
'Kodak' without delay. Life without a 'Kodak' is life writ in water.

Take a '**Kodak**' *with you*

'Take a "Kodak" with you', advertisement from *Punch*, 1928.

Kodak advertisement by Claude Shepperson, c.1924.

Booklet publicising the Post Office travel warrant service, 1930s.

Lloyds Bank foreign exchange leaflet, undated.

advertising that knowing a smatter of the language –

> ...takes you into the conversational atmosphere of the boulevard, the café and the plage.

Sky Tours suggested that although most hotel staff on the Continent spoke some English –

> It can be much more fun if you learn a few words and phrases of the local language. For a few shillings you can buy a simple language record and phrase book.

The Automobile Association published such a book in the 1930s, covering five languages and including phrases for when the car broke down, for camping and for making complaints!

And then, for those travelling abroad, besides packing the obvious passports, visas etc. there was the decision of how much money to take and in what form. Post-WWII restrictions of how much sterling could be taken would possibly not have affected those on cheaper packages who would have been unlikely to have had much spare cash anyway, but it did restrict others. A *Vogue* Nivea advertisement of 1960 advised –

> This year turn tan beautifully. Buy before you go. Save on your travel allowance. These things cost more abroad.

And for the less sophisticated there was a real fear as to what might happen if you lost your cash or if it were stolen; with credit cards almost unknown at the time, the travellers cheque provided a solution. Although Henry Gaze, an early Cook's rival, had offered travellers' cheques in the 1860s, it was Cook's that came to dominate this

AA Conversation Handbook, 1930s.

Insurance

It is important to remember that only Yugoslavia has a free Health Service like that of the United Kingdom so medical bills elsewhere have to be paid. You probably won't need such attention anyway but its well worth insuring against just in case. Then there's loss of baggage and personal belongings and loss of deposits. It's a thousand to one that you won't suffer such loss— but you'll enjoy your holiday much more if you know that a small premium has covered you against the risk. A Sky Tours Master Policy gives you full protection against Personal Accident, Medical and other expenses, Personal Baggage and Loss of Deposits for the modest premium of 20/-.

Baggage Allowance

Your free baggage allowance is usually 33 lbs. per person. You will see from the table shown here that you can pack a lot within the limit. In addition, you may take such items as your raincoat, handbag, lightweight reading material and a small camera. These are not included in the weight. Don't forget to make allowance for presents that you will be bringing home.

Make sure that your identifying labels are securely fixed to your case or bag and that they are clearly marked with your name and destination. As a safety precaution put a label *inside* the case with your name, full home address and holiday address on it.

Packing for the Holiday

It is surprising how much you can pack and still keep within your baggage allowance of 33 lbs. per person. Here are two packing lists as a rough guide when you are deciding what to take. You can adjust the lists to suit your needs. Each list totals 30 lbs., leaving another 3 lbs. for purchases which you will want to bring home. Remember, for example, that a bottle of wine can weigh as much as 1½ lbs.

For Men

	lbs.	ozs.
28 in. suitcase (empty)	6	8
1 lounge suit	4	15
1 sports jacket and trousers ..	4	0
1 pr. light shoes	1	8
1 pr. beach sandals		14
3 prs. pants and vests	1	8
6 shirts	2	2
2 prs. pyjamas	1	10
2 prs. shorts	1	8
2 ties		4
4 prs. socks		6
12 handkerchiefs		10
1 pullover		6
1 pr. bathing trunks & beach towel	1	4
1 lightweight dressing gown ..	1	9
toilet requisites	1	0
Total	**30 lbs.**	**0 ozs.**

For Women

	lbs.	ozs.
24 in. suitcase (empty)	5	8
2 prs. shoes & beach slippers ..	3	0
underwear	2	9
2 nightdresses/pyjamas		11
1 dressing gown	1	4
6 prs. stockings		8
1 swimsuit & beach towel ..	1	5
2 jumpers & 1 cardigan	1	4
1 skirt	1	4
1 suit	2	2
beachwear	1	0
2 dresses	3	2
2 cotton frocks	2	2
2 blouses		12
1 hat		4
12 handkerchiefs		5
sundry cosmetics & toilet requisites	3	0
Total	**30 lbs.**	**0 ozs.**

5

Money
ON HOLIDAY

Nobody likes to carry large sums in cash, but what else can you do?—You can make use this year of the services which the Westminster Bank provides for *everyone*, whether they are customers of the Bank or not.

If you are going abroad

Westminster Bank Travellers Cheques will solve most of your problems. They are obtainable on demand at all branches and are 'cashable' throughout the world. Your foreign currency requirements can be supplied, too—at short notice by any branch and on demand by some.

If you are staying in the U.K.

Travellers Cheques will again come to your aid. They are 'cashable' at banking offices in all parts of the British Isles and are often accepted by hotels and shops. And, of course, if you are a customer of the Bank, your own cheques can, by arrangement, be cashed in your holiday town.

WESTMINSTER BANK LIMITED

Above: Advertisement for Westminster Bank, undated.

Opposite page: Detailed guidance on packing for your holiday, from a Sky Tours brochure, undated.

market, and, indeed, in difficult economic climes, Cook's cheque operation was to keep the firm afloat. In the period covered by this book, although a number of banks, as the Westminster, also had something similar with warnings not to carry large sums in cash, Cook's advertisements dominated and very simply gave the advantages of the system – refunds if lost or stolen, refundable, and accepted everywhere.

Whilst packing, holiday makers had the fun of imagining what lay ahead, but, as has been shown, were bombarded with competing advertisements and advice, so the final decision was no small matter.

PLACES AND PLEASURES

The development of a town, village or hamlet into a holiday destination was frequently to do with health. Earlier on a site might acquire a reputation for being a place of healing by being associated with a saint, a holy relic, or the like; later by being near a well or spring of supposedly healing waters. By the seventeenth and eighteenth centuries Harrogate, Wells, Tunbridge and Epsom were flooded with visitors optimistically hoping that their complaints could at least be relieved if not cured by 'taking the waters'. It is arguable whether these early spas can be classed as holiday venues, but they did become an attraction as much for the socialising and entertainment that went on, as well as for their possible therapeutic potential.

The places that were to grow into holiday resorts continued to use 'health' in their publicity. 'Healthy Herne Bay', 'Fleetwood for Health and Pleasure', 'Hastings for Health' were typical headlines for posters, leaflets and brochures much of the following text resorting to medical flummery. Southend, once a small hamlet known only for its oysters and manufactured crystallised salt, in setting out its wares as a resort boasted –

> Pure sunlight of the ordinary intensity raises the antiseptic power of the blood and kills the germs of tuberculosis in 10 minutes.

Walton estimates that by WWI there were over one hundred seaside resorts vying for visitors, on the east coast – Scarborough and

Above: Poster publicising Brighton Carnival, Conrad Leigh, 1920s.

Left: Early twentieth century poster, Harrogate 'Britain's 100% Spa'.

TORQUAY
for SUNSHINE *and* SPA TREATMENTS

TORQUAY, with its splendid record of sunshine, its ultra-violet rays, and its warm western breezes, will do all that Nature can to make you well and happy. And those who need medical treatments to preserve or restore their health will find the Medical Baths perfectly equipped for every kind of treatment and cure. Torquay Medical Baths undoubtedly form one of the most up-to-date and luxurious modern spa establishments in Europe.

List of Spa Treatments available :

BALNEOLOGICAL.

Hot Sea Water, with Blanket Pack
Deep Bath
Seaweed Bath
Carbonic Acid Bath
Oxygen Bath
Vapour
Aix Douche-Massage
Vichy Douche-Massage
Pine Bath
Plombières (Intestinal Lavage)
Turkish Bath
Bourbon-Lancy Bath
Needle Spray
Sitz Douche
Scotch Douche
Sulphur Bath
Bran, Oatmeal or Soda Bath
Peat Bath and Packs
Brine Bath (Concentrated Sea Water)
Contrast Bath
Salt Rub
Iodine Bath
Nauheim Bath

ELECTRICAL.

Bristow Coil
Two or Four Cell Schnee Bath
Dowsing Radiant Heat
Electric Heat "Sun" Cabinet
Cataphoresis (Ionic Medication)
Diathermy (Electro-Thermal Penetration)
Electro-Vibro Massage
Electro Massage
Faradism, Galvanism or Sinusoidal
CURRENTS
High-Frequency Current
Ultra-Violet Rays (Artificial Sunshine)
(Carbon Arc or Mercury Vapour)

ACCESSORY.

Throat, Nose or Ear Irrigations
Liver Packs
Pistany Mud Packs
Dartmoor Peat Packs
Massage
Swedish Massage
Chiropody

NEW "VITA"-GLASS SUN LOUNGE—THE LARGEST IN THE BRITISH ISLES—OPEN EVERY DAY FOR ULTRA-VIOLET RADIATION.

All well-known British and Continental Spa Treatments administered on the most approved principles by fully qualified attendants, with accuracy and the utmost comfort. The charges are moderate.

TRAVEL SWIFTLY AND SMOOTHLY BY G.W.R. — TORQUAY MEDICAL BATHS

If you are interested, please write for complete informative literature to :
J. M. SCOTT, SPA DIRECTOR, TORQUAY.

Above: 'Torquay for sunshine and spa treatments' advert, *The London Illustrated News*, July 1929.

Right: 1930s advertisement for Weston Super-Mare stressing the benefits of ozone.

You Can't buy it!

"AIR LIKE WINE"

First-Class all-the-year-round Holiday Resort

Golf . Tennis . Bowls . Boating
Bathing . Fine Marine Lake
Magnificent New Dance Pavilion
Splendid Accommodation

ASK FOR TOURIST OR EXCURSION PROGRAMME AT LMS STATIONS AND TOURIST AGENCIES

Free Guide from :
F. PICKETT,
General Manager,
Advertising Association
(Department "L")

WESTON SUPER-MARE

Skegness; on the west – Blackpool and Southport; in the south-east – Southend, Margate, Ramsgate, Broadstairs and Eastbourne; to the south – Hastings, Brighton and Bournemouth; and in Wales and the southwest – Prestatyn, LLandudno, Rhyl and Torquay.

Each resort began to attract its own clientele, usually from the nearest manufacturing towns; the Lancashire cotton mill workers drifted to Blackpool, Cockneys to Southend, West Midland factory workers to Rhy and LLandudno. Much, of course, depended on the spread of the railways, so much so that some trains became known by the resorts they served, such as the Brighton Belle in 1934.

Resorts began to compete not only on the grounds as to which was the healthiest, but which could offer the most sumptuous or

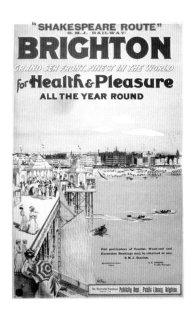

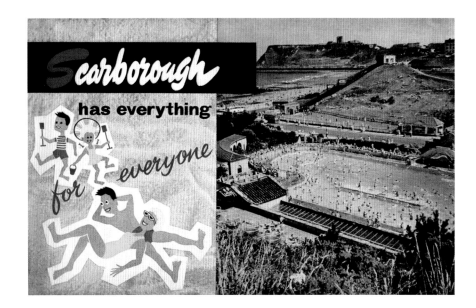

1930s programme for Blackpool's North Pier.

original attractions – places of entertainment, architectural wonders, activities and sports – each resort hyped these in their publicity as 'larger', 'more modern', 'technically most advanced' than any of their competitors. Promenades, built both to keep the sea at bay and to provide an area for strolling and for showing off one's holiday outfits, vied as to which was longer; piers, which had originally served for embarking and disembarking visitors and freight from boats, were refurbished and lengthened and adorned with sideshows and theatres, Southend able to boast the longest and with a railway, Blackpool the most, with three.

Many of the resorts set land aside for sideshows and slot machines and fairgrounds. Here competition might be as to which place had the most daring dipper, the smartest dodgem cars, or the most magnetic curiosity, as Blackpool getting holiday makers to pay to see Epstein's 'Jacob and the Angel' on the Golden Mile. These amusement areas took on a character of their own and often publicised themselves and their entertainments separately from publicity issued from the town hall. Blackpool's Pleasure Beach, Southend's Kursaal, and Margate's Dreamland, became attractions themselves irrespective of what else was on offer in the town. And when there were special events at the resort these could merit publicity of their own, as the illuminations at Morecombe and Blackpool. Carnivals in Brighton, or when an exceptional star of stage, screen or radio was featured in a show, as when Mae West played Diamond Lil at Blackpool's Opera House.

When it came to grand buildings of some architectural quality to show off about, Brighton had its Pavilion, as did Bexhill; Morecombe had its art deco hotel, but Blackpool again won hands down with the Tower, the Winter Gardens, the Opera House, the Grand Theatre and the Ice Drome. When architects such as Oliver Hill, Joseph Emberton,

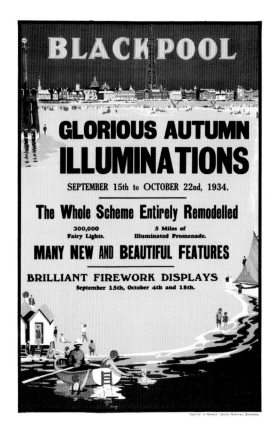

Above: 1934 poster for Blackpool's 'Glorius Autumn lluminations'.

Left: 1929 Souvenir Programme for Blackpool Winter Gardens and Opera House.

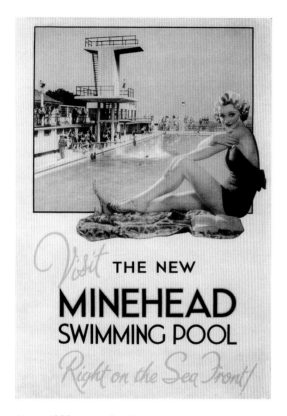

Above: 1930s poster for Minehead swimming pool, complete with modernist diving board.

Right: General pamphlet for entertainment at Southend & Westcliffe-on-Sea, 1962.

Above: Plan of Clacton Pier from holiday brochure, undated.

Above right: 'Fleetwood for Health & Pleasure', official guide, 1949.

and Mendelson & Charmayeff were commissioned for resort architecture, this would give the town publicity at a national level. A member of the Emberton team for Blackpool's Ice Drome and Pleasure Beach was Tom Purvis, one of the major commercial artists of the 1930s, who not only supplied spectacular posters and programmes but conjured up Mr. Sunshine, who became the Pleasure Beach's symbol for its publicity.

Few resort hotels were of the size and grandeur or had the finance to advertise themselves, certainly not at a national level, but information on them was usually included in civic brochures, where, accompanied by photographs, they always took precedence over mere boarding houses and other accommodation. Exceptions that

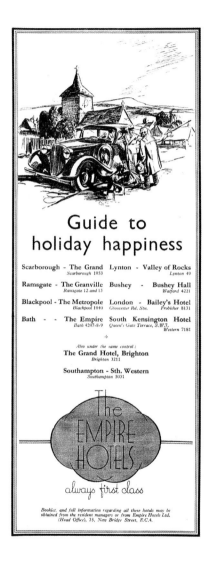

GLENEAGLES
HOTEL
P E R T H S H I R E

the
unique
Scottish
resort

Open from Easter
to the end of
October

*Enquiries for accommodation will receive the
personal attention of the Resident Manager*

Above: Advertisement for the Gleneagles Hotel, undated.

Opposite page, left: Wartime seaside publicity for Hastings and St Leonards, 1940.

Opposite page, right: General advertisement for the Empire chain of hotels, 1930s.

did use the national press were the Royal Hotel, Scarborough and the Imperial and Palace Hotels in Torquay. A 1935 press advertisement for the Torquay Palace boasted 'exclusive guests at inclusive prices' and hyped –

The Palace IS the Season – and the Riviera too.

Scotland, an area less frequently mentioned in histories of holiday making, had at least one hotel that advertised regularly and nationally – Gleneagles in Perthshire. Besides having 'Championship, King's, Queen's and 9-hole 'wee' golf courses', it was to offer tennis, squash, croquet, swimming, dancing, film shows, and, private cars to meet its guests at Gleneagles station. Where hotels were part of chains they could afford to advertise widely. A group such as the Empire Hotels, in the 1930s advertised regularly in *Punch* the 'holiday happiness' that was to be found in its Grand in Scarborough, its Granville in Ramsgate and in its Metropole at Blackpool.

Holiday borough's advertising was limited by finance, as the government was generally against money collected in the rates (former council tax) being spent on such frivolity, the government, itself, only in the early stages of its' learning of the importance of publicity. Most holiday resorts before 1921 had had to rabble rouse local entrepreneurs to contribute, on a voluntary basis, for civic publicity, and generally such contributions fell far short of what was needed. An exception was Hastings & St. Leonards, which had had an 'advertising association' from the 1880s and reported in *Art & Industry* in 1949 that in this early period it was sometimes able to raise as much as £1500 in any one year.

A 1921 Act of Parliament eased the situation a little by allowing resorts to use 'profits from entertainments' for advertising; and overtime the act was extended so that even a small proportion of the rates could be so used. In 1948 Hastings reported that it had raised £9000 within the regulations, and £6000 from voluntary contributions.

Some resorts entered into joint advertising schemes with the railway companies. The designs had to be approved by local councils which tended to be conservative when it came to aesthetics, resulting often, as some critics would have it, with resorts coming across as 'worthy but dull'. The LNER (London & North Eastern Railways) alone refused to accept resort vetoes, asserting that posters appearing on its stations were the responsibility of its Advertising Manager. And this resulted in its inter-war posters being some of the most iconic in advertising history. It was in the interest of all railway companies to 'show-off' their destinations, so the Great Western boosted the

Right: Advertisement for the Imperial Torquay, 'The English Hotel in the Mediterranean Manner', 1953.

Opposite page, left: Brochure cover for 'Plymouth – Delightful Centre for Holidays', 1955.

Opposite page, right: Herne Bay brochure cover, Geo (George) Ayling, undated.

The spot to be in

Life has 'Continental' charm at the Imperial, Torquay. Tropical palms, blue skies, your own sunny beach, tennis, squash . . . or just relax in the luxury of Europe's finest seashore hotel. Write for Brochure BH.

The *Imperial* TORQUAY

The ENGLISH HOTEL in the MEDITERRANEAN MANNER

Price: One Shilling

PLYMOUTH
DELIGHTFUL CENTRE FOR HOLIDAYS

HERNE BAY

THE OFFICIAL PUBLICATION OF
THE URBAN DISTRICT COUNCIL.

Prince Regent travelling to Brighton,
*The Official Handbook of the
Corporation of Brighton*, cover by
Aubrey Hammond, 1939.

BOURNEMOUTH

Bournemouth brochure cover, 1965.

Cornish Riviera, the Southern Railway covered resorts from Ramsgate to Plymouth, London, Midland & Scottish covered those from Southend to the Lakes via Blackpool, and LNER those from Clacton to Aberdeen.

Most resorts, besides posters and press advertisements, would issue leaflets and brochures, some of the latter running to over 200 pages. Leaflets would be no more than a couple of pages or a folded large page, tempting potential visitors to contact the town hall for more information. A Southend and Westcliff-on-Sea leaflet for 1962 was just a folded sheet, but had a very simple yet striking black and yellow image of sunbathers in deck chairs on the outer side, and within, lists of attractions, amenities, and special events – from the Pier Department's Horticultural Group's Chrysanthemum Show to the Illuminations.

Early resort brochures tended to be large and pompous, as Southend's for 1924, a tome of some 230 pages, which not only provided holiday makers with some hundred pages listing hotel and boarding accommodation, but a potted history of the Borough from 894 (the Battle of Benfleet), the health advantages of staying there, train timetables and fares, along with such unique items as lists of public conveniences, police telephone boxes, and Jewish restaurants. And, unlikely to have been found in any Lancashire resort brochure, sections in French, German, Dutch, Italian, Spanish and Portuguese.

Although such tomes were not possible in the rationing of paper and print during and after WWII, by 1965 Bournemouth was yet again publishing one of over 200 pages. And soon after the war, Hastings, which had been so go-ahead when it came to funding its publicity in the early twentieth century, actually employed a rarity, a publicity manager – one W.H. Dyer – who boasted of some nine publications issuing from his department –

– a general 'throw-away' folder
– a larger superior folder 'Round-about Hastings'
– a coloured map
– a booklet for conference secretaries
– a winter season folder
– a folder listing forthcoming events
– a 'Plan your day, plan your week-end' folder
– a complete Accomodation Register
– a souvenir booklet for visiting parties

Writing in 1949, Dyer advised councils to focus on an overall publicity policy and to leave the actual design and format of it to a good advertising agency. In the post-war years Hastings seems to have used

S.H. Benson and to have commissioned some of the major commercial artists of the time as Eric Fraser. And Hastings was one of the few resorts to develop a publicity 'character' as Mr. Therm for the Gas Board, or Bertie Bassett for liquorice allsorts – one Happy Harold – 'a cheerful, cockney little Saxon', designed and drawn by Bruce Angrave, an artist and sculptor who also produced posters for the railways, both pre- and post-war, for resorts, as Cromer and Blackpool.

Along with actual resort towns were the holiday camps, often more noisy in their publicity, but actually only ever taking up a small part of the holiday industry. The concept of bringing people together for shared activities, away from their normal round-the-year existence, initially stemmed from idealism rather than commercialism, and as 'idealism' usually attracted limited finance, the activities and

Advertisement for the first Butlin's Holiday Camp, Skegness, 1936.

accommodation tended to be simple (frequently tented). For children and adolescents there was, of course, scout and guide camping, but other providers of 'holiday camps' were such organisations as the Band of Hope, the Woodcraft Folk and then the Youth Hostelling Association. The Holiday Fellowship initially ran camps for the young, but soon was acquiring centres across the country having 'beautiful locations, great leaders and pleasant sociable evenings'.

Some of the early camps were associated with 'leftish' bodies as those run by Co-operative Associations, Trade Unions and labour movements. A Socialist Holiday Camp was founded at Caister as early as 1906; and both local and national Co-operative Societies were running camps from the 1910s. The Civil Service Union had set up its own camping association in 1924. All of this was long before one, Billy Butlin, came on the scene in 1936, when he set up his first 'holiday camp' in Skegness. Butlin, born in South Africa and brought up in Canada had relatives in the fairground business in Britain. Having visited them when serving with the Canadian Army in France in WWI, he joined them in 1921, purchasing a hoop-la stall for himself.

From such modest beginnings Butlin's empire grew, initially with amusement parks, and even zoos, at various seaside sites around the country. Getting to appreciate the misery of families on holiday, barred from their boarding houses in all weathers, Butlin decided to branch out with centres where accommodation, catering and entertainment all took place 'under one roof' as it were. Starting with Skegness, Butlin was eventually to develop some nine sites, delayed in his entrepreneurial ambitions only by the onset of war. His wartime experience, as Director General of Hostels for the government, gave him both a better understanding of what visitors might need, along with a government subsidy to finance his expansion.

Advertisement for Butlin's '£100 000 Luxury Holiday Camps' at Skegness and Clacton on Sea, c.1938.

General Butlin's press advertisement, 'Butlin's, For a Real Family Holiday', 1950s.

The enterprise that staggered the Holiday World

Butlin's £100 000 LUXURY HOLIDAY CAMPS

SKEGNESS & CLACTON ON SEA
DOVERCOURT BAY
associated with Butlins

Butlin's FOR A REAL FAMILY HOLIDAY

There's pure enjoyment for every member of the family at Butlin's, where they will all have a wonderful time among the finest array of entertainments, amusements and amenities obtainable anywhere — and all included in the All-in Tariff. In your sleeping chalet at the edge of the sea and in your dining hall you are surrounded with service. At Butlin's you do no more for yourself than you would expect to do at any first-class hotel. Bring the family to Butlin's this year and you'll all enjoy a real holiday!

BUTLIN'S LTD.
439 OXFORD STREET, LONDON, W.I

TRAVEL BY
BRITISH RAILWAYS

Pre-war advertisement for Butlin's,
'The Best holiday we've ever had'.

Modest timber chalets with cold water and a shared outside tap for hot water, morphed into bathrooms between chalets, and, eventually, provision en suite. And soon there were few sports and social activities that could not be found at a Butlin's somewhere or other, along with endless competitions from knobbly knees to glamorous grandmothers. Butlin would continuously make trips abroad, frequently to America, to pick up new ideas for both services and amusements.

When it came to advertising and publicity Butlin was a maestro. He is quoted as saying –

...strike a lucky idea, sell the people something they need and wrap it in cellophane.

And 'wrap it in cellophane' he did! From the start he was advertising his Skegness venture nationally in the Sunday Express. And soon the catchphrases were cascading out of his Oxford Street Head Office –

'The Enterprise that staggered the Holiday World'
'Holidays with Play! Nothing extra to Pay'
'Happy children mean happy parents, mean happy holidays.'
'Where Holidays are Jollydays'
'Luxury holidays within the reach of Everyone'

There was not a publicity or advertising trick that Butlin missed. Firstly, he saw that his name was everywhere – on every camp facility, on every keepsake in the camp gift shops, on every postcard sent by his campers to their kith and kin. And Butlin would scheme to associate his camps with the 'great and the good' – he had the cricketer Len Hutton judge beauty contests, Prince Philip call in at

60

Above: Assorted Holiday Camp badges from Butlin's Skegness, Middleton Tower, and Warner's.

Above right: Brochure for Bramble's Holiday Camp on the Isle of Wight, 1951.

Pwllheli (where Philip had been posted during the war), Sir Harry Lauder open the Scottish camp at Ayr, and well-known singers and comedians perform at his Sunday night concerts. Butlin brought his name to London with camp reunions, dances and funfairs at Earls Court and Olympia. And to gain further brownie points he got his camps associated with good causes – 'Celebrity Sundays' in aid of Great Ormond Street Hospital, accommodation for the Lions Club annual children's games, car raffles for the National Playing Fields Association, and so on. Besides the excellent publicity this provided, it also earned him a knighthood in 1964.

There were a number of smaller holiday camp enterprises, both before and alongside Butlins, drowned out by his noise. Brambles, at

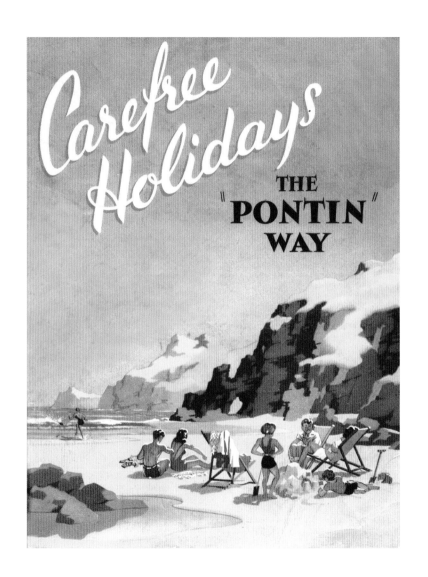

Above: 1950s advertisement for Squires Gate Holiday Camp, Blackpool.

Opposite page, left: Assorted Butlin's badges from the 1940s and 1950s.

Opposite page, right: Brochure for Pontin's holiday camps, 'The Pontin Way', undated.

Freshwater on the Isle of Wight, although only taking five hundred holidaymakers compared to Butlin's thousands, nevertheless was able to offer a large number of activities including roller skating, table tennis and whist drives with a ballroom sporting 'the finest possible marble floor'. A 1951 brochure assured campers –

Outdoor life at a Camp after the noisy streets of the town soon brings colour back to the cheek and the spontaneous friendship of other campers quickly helps one to think that life after all is worth living.

The holiday camps that were to come to rival those of Butlin were those of Fred Pontin. Brought up in a family of East End cabinet- makers, Pontin broke away to become a stock-broking jobber, and, at one time, to run a football pool. Medically barred from war service he, as Butlin, helped run workers hostels during the war. Based on this experience he started to buy up former army bases, now disused, to develop into holiday camps. His first was at Brean Sands, near Burnham-on-Sea, which he personally ran with what has been described as 'an iron fist'. Encouraged by the success of this he bought up further camps and the Pontin empire rapidly expanded. In 1963 he launched Pontinental, and soon there were Pontin camps, now called 'holiday villages', along the Mediterranean coastline from Spain/Majorca/Ibiza to Greece and Yugoslavia. Although services and entertainments at a Pontin's camp had much that was similar to those of Butlin, with 'blue-coats' instead of 'red-coats', they were a tinge less sophisticated in some ways, as with impromptu concerts and sing songs; yet in other ways they were ahead, providing self-catering accommodation and self-service restaurants some time before Butlin's came round to the ideas. Fred Pontin, was temperamentally the opposite of Butlin – a taciturn man of few words, avoiding the limelight. Yet by his own empire building and low-key charity work, especially for theatrical good causes, he too was knighted, in 1976.

Meanwhile, a totally different kind of camping holiday was becoming popular – either tenting or caravanning on camping sites. Camping, (the first commercial camping site had opening in the 1890s) was to prove one of the cheapest ways of holidaying. By 1910 a National Camping Club had been established, aided in its evangelism for the simple pleasures of a tented holiday by Baden-Powell becoming its President.

A NEW WAY TO HAPPINESS .
GO CARAVANNING

If you have yet to learn the joys and freedom of Trailer Caravanning, send for the Eccles catalogue, consider the grace and beauty, the luxurious completeness, and the modest cost of Eccles caravanning. Then let us tell you where you can see a full range of models—and judge for yourself. There is an Eccles service Agent near you — ready to help you get the most out of—

ECCLES

fbl.

ECCLES MOTOR CARAVANS Ltd., 130 - 138 Hazelwell Lane, Stirchley Birmingham

Opposite page: Cover of a booklet publicising Grouville Holiday Camp, Jersey, 1936.

Right: Eccles Motor Caravans, advertisement for streamlined caravans, undated.

But caravanning, as compared to tent camping, was to grow into an altogether more comfortable, even sophisticated, means of holidaying. Before the twentieth century horse-drawn caravans had been the province of gypsies, showmen, travelling preachers, and the like; sometimes taken up by Bohemian types, such as Augustus John, the artist, and some equally eccentric aristocrats. When the Birmingham based company Eccles, produced its first 'motor-home' in 1919, the first order came from one, the Dowager Countess Rhonda. The early caravans were not cheap, being hand-produced. To drum

CARAVANNING AND CAMPING

Issued by
THE AUTOMOBILE ASSOCIATION,
FANUM HOUSE,
NEW COVENTRY STREET,
Secretary. LONDON W.1. Telephone,
Sir Stenson Cooke Whitehall 1200.
Membership Exceeds Half a Million.

4TH EDITION

YOUTH HOSTELS ASSOCIATION (ENGLAND & WALES)

Handbook

1955

YHA

PRICE NINEPENCE   POST FREE ELEVENPENCE

up trade to the lower classes the firm produced sales brochures declaring 'The Holiday Problem Solved' whoever you are.

Eccles were to dominate the caravan market in the inter-war years, initially constructing its caravans on car chassis, but soon producing aerodynamic art deco type designs to be pulled separately by cars, at that time limited, for safety, to 10 m.p.h. A Caravan Club had been started, even earlier than the one for camping, in 1907, but it wasn't really until the 1920s and 30s, when Eccles took to mass-production, and the speed limit for a car pulling a caravan was increased to 40 m.p.h. that caravanning became a widespread, relatively cheap, and a considerably independent way of holidaying. Most of the sites were small family run enterprises, the first municipally owned site was actually not opened until the 1960s.

The 'green and pleasant land' that had been Britain, through the growth of the holiday industry had become littered with sites offering a variety of attractions for holiday breaks. Walton estimated that there was not a gap of more than ten miles along Britain's coastline lacking a holiday destination of one sort or another. Publicised initially for the healthiness given by being in the open air, in natural surroundings, exposed to the the sun and the sea, resorts were increasingly to be advertised for more carnal attractions as sheer fun and possibly 'romance'. British holiday resort advertising always had an unrestrained light-heartedness to it, as so it should have, yet curiously it rarely went as far as to make use of humour, part and parcel of fun, humour which was so in vogue, even for such potentially 'unhumourless' products as oil and petrol, in the advertising of the time.

AGENTS AND PACKAGES

In her book on working class tourism Susan Barton provides a most comprehensive definition of the 'package holiday' –

> ...a combination or package of transport, accommodation and perhaps some other recreational services which is sold at a single all-inclusive price. The price is usually substantially lower than could be obtained by conventional methods of booking transport and accommodation separately with individual tariffs. Normally the tourist travels in a group with other travellers. The consumer has the convenience of buying a single ticket. Through bulk purchase of the components of the holiday the tour operator is able to secure a lower price than would be available to individual travellers. The volume of demand means transport providers can rely on a high load factor, that is all or almost all seats on transport filled, allowing costs per passenger to be reduced.

The name Thomas Cook immediately springs to mind; but 'packages' were around before Cook's start up and the company was not alone in its development of packaged holidays. The history of holidaymakers choosing to let someone else organise their lives for a short time is rich and complex, including transportation by camels and horses to flying by jets, and extending to most countries across the world.

Holiday historians suggest that Thomas Cook was 'performing on a crowded stage', yet few names of early rivals, or even

LUNNS 1950 HOLIDAYS

Above: Cover of a travel booklet for Dean & Dawson, design by Eric Sandon, 1934.

Right: Nostalgic lake scene for Lunn's brochure, 1950.

predecessors are ever given. One that crops up occasionally is that of Henry Gaze. Gaze, first operating from Southampton and then from London, was, as Cook, a non-conformist and equally entrepreneurial. As a classy boot and shoemaker (to Queen Victoria and Napoleon III), he was used to travelling to and from Paris on business and began taking parties along with him; soon beyond France to the Holy Land. He wrote popular guidebooks to many European countries which, in their turn, publicised his tours; and returning from trips he would lay on extravagant multi-media entertainments telling of his travels which also served to attract potential customers. He, as Cook and Cook's son, John, had commercial links to a number of railway companies, acting as agent for both London & South Western and London & North Western operations.

However, Gaze's company was bankrupt by the turn of the century, by which time another of Cook's rivals, Henry Lunn, had launched his Co-operative Educational Tours. Lunn was at the other end of the 'package' market to Cook, his early tours only open to private and public school students, to undergraduates and to service officers. The 'class' focus of Lunn's market continued when, with his passion for skiing, Lunn founded The Public Schools Alpine Sports Club in 1903 and The Alpine Ski Club in 1908, the latter being a kind of gentlemen's club for skiers and mountaineers. Lunn is thought to have provided the first winter sports packages in 1898, at Chamonix and Klosters, which were to grow into major resorts, both for package holidays and for independent travellers. Lunn was, as Cook and Gaze, an evangelical non-conformist (in his case an ordained minister) as well as being a qualified doctor. As a consequence, his tours, in addition to their various appeals to the well-heeled, had spiritual and health aspects to them, along with such physical activities as skating, skiing and climbing. Lunn's was to go through hard times, especially

70

during the depression when Henry's brother, George, resorted to massive advertising to try to avert disaster; however, the name Lunn lived on, merging with the Polytechnic Touring Company in 1962 to become Lunn Poly.

The Polytechnic Touring Company also had educational roots evolving out of Quinton Hogg (the founder of Regent Street Polytechnic), giving both his students and his staff holidays in his own home. As Lunn's, it began exclusively for educational groups, but it too, eventually, opened its doors to the general public. From the 1880s it was organising packages to the Continent and to specific events, as

Above left: Press advertisement for WTA, as featured in the Kodak magazine, 1937.

Above centre: Brochure cover for the Polytechnic Touring Association created by advertising agents Pritchard, Wood & Partners, 1938.

Above right: Poster for Thomas Cook, design by Derrick Ashby, 1957.

the Paris Exhibition and the Chicago World Fair. The Company would retain its links to the Polytechnic, having an office adjacent, right through to the 1950s.

The organisation that was, perhaps, to be an altogether more serious competitor to Thomas Cook when it came to package holidays, was the Workers' Travel Association (WTA), born from the Trade Union and Co-operative movements, and also with an educational aim, that of internationalism. A 'non-profit' organisation, it offered affordable overseas package holidays to working class folk, additionally helping the progress of international solidarity along by providing prior language classes for its would-be travellers. But whoever else entered the package market it was Thomas Cook that was to become the market leader. Although Thomas is given most of the credit, and it is his name that the company carries, it was actually his son John, the realist, who grounded the firm, gave it gravity – who helped it survive. For Thomas was an idealist, an evangelist, who, although he was quite capable of making tough deals and getting the planning and detail right, let his heart, or rather his spirit, overrule his head.

Cook's early tours were energised by his religious zeal and temperance, keeping people away from the evils of drink and showing them that they could lead a finer life guided by the Lord and free of alcohol. His modest first 'package', taking people from Leicester to Loughborough by train, for a temperance meeting, was followed not long afterwards by an altogether more ambitious package, taking literally hundreds to the Great Exhibition in London in 1851. Not only did Cook arrange the rail transport but he rented property on a temporary basis, to provide accommodation for his voyagers. By 1855 he was running packages to the Continent; by the 1860s to the Middle East. In Egypt the Company came to hold such sway that it was virtually seen to be an arm of the British Government. By the 1880s son John had taken over the running of the business and was accompanying 'packages' to the United States. In 1910 the firm was able to brag in its advertising –

> There are spots on the sun but not one spot on earth you cannot visit with the aid of a Cook's ticket.

Thomas Cook had its ups and downs, John's sons, Ernest and Frank, not quite matching the calibre of their forebears. Although events

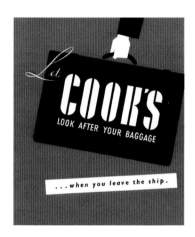

Above: Cook's brochure for its ship travel tours, 'Let Cook's look after your baggage when you leave the ship', 1950s.

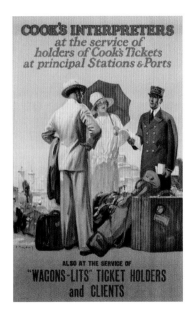

Cook's poster by F. Gardner, 1928.

such as the growth of holiday camps, competition from the airlines, its merging with the Belgian company Wagons-Lits, its short-term nationalisation during which it ran as a state enterprise, and the Suez crisis, all affected Cook's trading position over the years, its name was forever in the public eye; it was to become the largest travel agency in the world.

Thomas Cook may have been something of a dreamer but he understood the key role advertising and publicity could have for his business and exploited it as well as he could. His adage was: 'Advertising is to trade what steam is to machinery.' He had had experience as a onetime printer and had written numerous tracts on religious and temperance concerns, and the 'package' company now began selling itself through as many means as available – leaflets, brochures, posters, and press advertisements; Cook was to publish what is believed to be the first travellers newspaper, to become known as the 'Traveller's Express'. There were major differences, between father and son, as to the focus of such publicity, for Thomas was all for the masses, whereas John wanted the firm to go upmarket, using such tags as: 'Select First-class Party of Limited Numbers.'

A slightly superior thread seems to have remained in some of Cook's advertising through to the post-WWII years. An example, possibly taking a swipe at the holiday camp movement as well as at its 'package' competitors was –

> ...a select clientele whose special requirements differ from those of the more popular holiday tour clients, who do not ask for the same detailed attention.

Post war, Cook's also publicised its 'packages' and other services by travel 'roadshows', attracting thousands to its film showings; and then

Above: Poster publicising Cook's conducted Tours, undated.

Left: Early Cook's poster featuring Queen Nefertiti,
'Nile & Palestine Arrangements', 1925.

Above left: Dean & Dawson 'Holidays Abroad' brochure, 1950.

Above right: Thomas Cook brochure with the very same image in colour, 1950s.

it pioneered retail 'travel' shops. By the 1960s there was barely an urban high street that did not feature a Thomas Cook.

Cook's poster and press advertising largely paralleled what was going on at the more conservative end of advertising and publicity at the time, not a hint of 'modernism' in sight. Mainly featured were smiling middle class tourists viewing the scenery, sometimes it would have no illustrations at all but just texts detailing the various packages on offer. Generally, Cook's advertising could be described as conventional for the industry with just a very occasional flash of originality as in a Haas designed cute advertisement showing a stack of children's letter blocks spelling COOKS, with just the three words 'Look mummy – TRAVEL'. Dean & Dawson, which was to merge with Cook's, shared some of its advertising but under its own name, sometimes with the self-same image, as in the 1950s, a brochure cover for Dean & Dawson headed 'Synopsis of Holidays Abroad' and an advertisement for Cook's with an alternative wording: 'The Perfect Holiday Abroad'.

Although eventually Cook's packages used every means of transport available, its early years were rail based. With the development of the combustion engine, other competitors now entered the market offering 'packages' by road. Charabancs (early coaches with wooden seats) were relatively short-lived for road touring, not around much beyond the 1920s, albeit the word persisted through to WWII as people would recount going on 'a charabanc' outing. Coach touring started soon after the first motorcars were on the roads. Crosville, at one time one of the largest coach firms offering 'package holidays, actually started off manufacturing cars in Chester in 1906, but by 1909 it was running a local bus service and this it built on with its tours. A number of other coach tour companies started in this way, as local bus services, as Southdown's operating out of Brighton and Royal Blue from Bournemouth. Shearings started out as a haulier and removal business in Oldham; whilst Wallace Arnold in Leeds started out directly offering tours, both becoming major operators in the coach tour business.

Coaches were initially used just as a cheaper way of getting to a holiday destination than by rail. This developed into a service where not only were holiday makers taken to their hotel by coach, but they also had on offer daily sightseeing trips from the hotel; such a service

Poster for Crosville Conducted Tours in Scotland & Yorkshire, 1938.

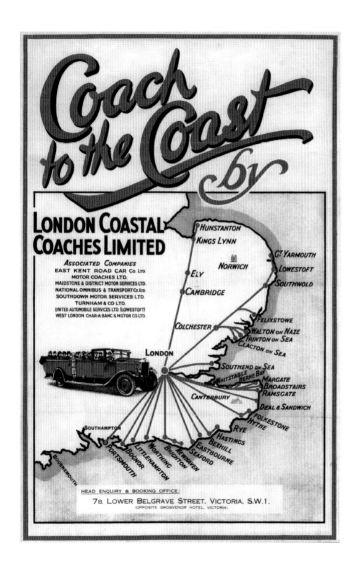

Above: Poster for United Automobile Services, design by Harry Stevens, 1957.

Left: Early coach poster for London Coastal Coaches Limited showing an image of a charabanc and its routes from London to the coast, undated.

came to be known in the holiday trade as 'fantail'. Eventually some coach firms began to offer a complete 'package' with tours around Great Britain, and then into Europe, as Shearings did just before the onset of WWII. And Shearings were the first coach company to restart Continental tours after the war, to be joined by some of its pre-war competitors and some new boys.

Holiday 'packages' by coach expanded rapidly in the 1950s and 60s. Victoria Coach Station, which had previously had its 'touring' offices tucked away, promoted them to the ground floor, putting out a general publicity leaflet 'Carefree Holidays by Coach'. By 1956 Fairways was running 26 motor coach tours across Europe, from

Below: Wallace Arnold coach tour brochure, 1960.

Below right: General poster publicising tours from Victoria Coach Station, design by Harry Stevens, c.1959.

Horizon

AIR-COACH LEISURE TOURS

GIVE YOU TWO HOLIDAYS IN ONE

Spain to Scandinavia and Yugoslavia, lasting from 10 to 32 days and of two classes – 'luxury' and 'popular'. A Dean & Dawson 1950 advertisement described its coach 'packages' –

> ...with overnight stays at most interesting places, time for leisure, good hotels and a luxurious coach, you can tour Europe in any direction – the capital cities, the provincial towns and the delightful ever-changing scenery.

Horizon Holidays, which by the 1960s, was selling air-coach tours described its coaches as 'the latest and best in Europe' –

> The armchairs are deeply sprung, roomy and with plenty of leg room. Ventilation is carefully and constantly controlled. The windows reaching right up to the roof and stretching from end to end of the coach are planned to give you maximum visibility... Every Horizon Coach has a microphone system so that our representative can tell you everything that's interesting about every place you pass. And every Horizon driver has been picked because he's superb at his job.

In the post-WWII years package holidays were using most types of available transport in a variety of combinations. Cook's offered the odd 'air' package even before the war, to Cannes in 1939. But it was the early post-war years that saw the full emergence of the 'by air' package holiday that was so seriously to affect the, by then, lack-lustre British seaside resorts.

A number of maverick entrepreneurs came on the scene making use of surplus planes and underemployed pilots, pioneered in this by Horizon Holidays. Started by a Reuter journalist, Vladimir Raitz,

Opposite page: Brochure for Horizon Air-Coach Leisure Tours, undated.

Above: 'Suggestions for your Holidays',
Swans Tours brochure, 1957.

Above right: Brochure for Fourways,
Continental Motor Coach Tours, 1956.

it cashed in not only on the planes and the pilots, but the whole
romance of how both had contributed to Britain's survival. Raitz
chartered his first plane in 1950 for a two-week package to Corsica;
and although, on a straightened budget, necessitating the use of
tents rather than hotels, he had some three hundred takers in his
first season.

Universal Sky Tours got to grips with the budgetary
limitations by flying its planes back-to-back, ensuring maximum
occupancy, and took hotels for whole seasons at much reduced

82

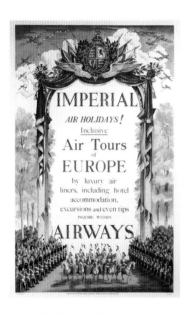

Above: 'Air Tours of Europe', poster for Imperial Airways, 1937.

prices, even buying hotels itself in Benidorm (where Franco in dire need of income was subsidising tourism). Soon Clarkson's were offering similar air packages via Luton airport to destinations across Europe to Greece. Even the well-established but more cautious W.T.A. had entered the air package business by 1955, Henry Lunn's and the Polytechnic Touring Company following suit. Thomson's did not really become a major player in the air package business until the mid-1960s, by which time it had absorbed some of its likely competitors, as Universal, and had the benefit of economy of scale with the arrival of Boeing's 737.

In all this enterprise, the companies were handicapped by the government's protective practices relating to BEA and BOAC, flying regular services to many of the same destinations as the package agents, and determined to protect their prices. Yet agents, such as Horizon, were nevertheless able to use cheapness as a sales line in their advertising, as usually their inclusive price for a whole package would be less than an individually booked standard flight fare. And, of course, much was made in publicity of speed compared to trying to reach the same destinations by road, rail or sea.

CRUISING

Cruising has always punched above its weight when it comes to what is considered the most romantic and sophisticated form of holidaying. For the majority of people their idea of what was involved in cruising was rarely from first-hand experience but more from Mills & Boon type novelettes and from Hollywood films such as 'Now Voyager'. In fact, for the years covered by this book, cruising was a near insignificant part of the tourist industry when it came to actual numbers. The index to Susan Barton's book on working class holidaying lacks the words 'cruise' or 'cruising'. Cruising was for the affluent and leisured classes, out of reach of the means of most people.

In the 1920s Percy Bradshaw in his tome on advertising art wrote of cruising –

> British shipping companies will tell you that there is comparatively little demand for World Tours or other lengthy and necessarily expensive pleasure cruises in this country, whereas, on the other hand, Americans not only have the 'cruise habit' but, what is much more important, the cruise MONEY!

The idea of being on a ship for any length of time just to relax and be entertained would have seemed quite strange much before the latter part of the nineteenth century. Ships were there for fishing, for carrying freight, and for people who needed to get from one place to another. Sailing was a hazardous and often unpleasant business and

ORIENT LINE CRUISES
20000 TON STEAMERS

Above: Poster for Orient Line Cruises, design by
Kate Burrell of The Clement Dane Studio, c.1930.

Left: 1930's poster for Orient Cruises, design
by Andrew Johnson.

Above: Royal Mail Line poster, 'New Winter Cruise', design by Percy Padden, 1934.

Left: Royal Mail Line brochure, design by Shep, 1927, Baynard Press.

Opposite page: P&O 'Winter Cruise' brochure, 1933.

A WINTER CRUISE
to the
WEST INDIES
and
SOUTH AMERICA
by
P & O
VICEROY of INDIA
20,000 TONS
Dec.29-Feb.12-1933-4

facilities on board basic. When steamships arrived with the potential to improve conditions, they were initially much reviled by a number of shipping companies as dirty and unreliable.

Unravelling the development of the cruising industry is not unlike trying to unravel macramé – shipping companies offering cruises were bought out, split, merged, demerged, chartered ships from each other, changed names, and disappeared; cruising ships were sold to and fro between companies, laid up, refurbished, given different colours and different names when used for different purposes, and registered under different flags at different times.

Rare examples of early attempts to open cruising to the less well off came from such agencies as the Co-operative Cruising Company,

and the Polytechnic Touring Company, both, at one time or another, offering budget price cruises to Norway and the Fjords; the Travel Savings Association (linked to the Union Castle Line) acted as a savings club and agent for cruises.

From the start there was some confusion as to actually what was meant by the word 'cruise'. A days' trip up the Scottish coast or round the Norfolk Broads, or from London down the Thames to Southend and beyond were all advertised as 'cruises'; as was travelling on a Fyffe banana boat to the Caribbean with perhaps a couple of nights ashore before travelling back home. Donald Meek listed five types of cruises, and although, as with most lists, there are omissions, his classification gives a flavor as to why and how cruising developed –

For sight-seeing	*very much an Edwardian pre-occupation*
For education	*as offered by the British Indian Line and others, with 'learning' schedules for students*
Reality cruising	*on freight boats where the crew had relatively little interest in the passengers*
Escapist cruising	*to be cocooned with all needs met on board*
Indulgence cruising	*as with the American 'booze' cruises during prohibition*

It is debatable as to when the first 'cruises' were launched and by which companies. It is recorded that P&O had passenger cruises as early as 1844, and in the 1880s had its 'Vectis' cruising both to

Above: Poster publicising two-hour 'cruises' to the Norfolk Broads.

Left: Poster publicising steamer trips from London to various seaside resorts, design by Harry Hudson Rodmell.

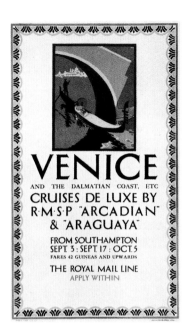

Royal Mail Line advertisement, design by Austin Cooper, 1926.

Norway and to the Mediterranean. The 'Ceylon' launched by the Oceanic Yachting Company is frequently quoted as the first cruiser, but the first actual dedicated cruise ship has been claimed by the Hamburg Amerika Line. And certainly the Scots were early on the scene, Nick Robins quoting an 1898 advertisement from one company –

> The vessels of this company were the first to begin cruises between Scotland and Norway and are of a convenient size to safely navigate the coast and fjords. The saloons are light and airy and are lighted by electricity. Hot and cold baths are provided. A full staff of stewards and stewardesses are carried, and the cuisine is equal to that of a first-class hotel. A Superintendent accompanies each vessel and arranges for shore excursions, so as to relieve passengers of personal trouble.

Cartwright and Harvey carry a quote that whoever actually started 'cruising' it was the British who – 'perfected it, expanded it, set shipboard standards and made it popular.' By the beginning of WWI most of the large shipping companies, operating from British ports, were offering cruises of one kind or another, the main players being the Royal Mail Steam Packet Company, P&O and Cunard. Yet at the time there were no more than a handful of ships that had actually been designed with cruising in mind. Most of the shipping was carrying government mail, administrators and military, along with freight and some passengers in transit. The shipping lines were subsidised for carrying out government business.

What the lines stumbled upon was the possibility of keeping afloat, as it were, by using their fleets for pleasure cruising in off-peak and slack periods. As early as 1894 it is recorded that the 'Princess

Victoria' had its cargo space fitted with temporary accommodation for 'yachting'. The Royal Mail Line in a 1927 brochure for cruises on its dedicated 'Arcadia' boasted –

> Not for her is the liner's round of ferrying passengers and cargo along a well-worn highway of the sea, with an occasional spell snatched for cruising when business needs grow less insistent.

Even after WWII when lines were replenishing their fleets Nick Robins wrote of Cunard and Canadian Pacific that none of their new ships

Right: Cover of a Canadian Pacific Railway Cruise folder, design by Tom Purvis, 1937.

Far right: Poster for Canadian Pacific, '9-Day Cruises', design by Tom Purvis, undated.

were built for sunshine cruises yet most of them were obliged to spend most of their working lives as cruise ships; at that time P&O, which was busy with the emigrant trade to Australia, had its emigrant ships summer cruising.

Certainly Norway and its fjords were the most popular destinations for early cruising; but then each line tended to develop cruising programme round its regular routes – the Orient Line and P&O, going eastward to the Mediterranean and beyond, The Royal Mail to the Caribbean, Union Castle to Africa and the south. For example, a typical cruising agenda for P&O's flagship the Viceroy of India in the mid-1930s was –

May: Greece and Egypt
June: Spain, Portugal and Monte Carlo
July: Casablanca, Las Palmas, Madeira and Teneriffe
August: Algiers, Italy, Spain

Cruising was to boom relatively, in the 20s and 30s, and the various shipping companies would compete, in their launch brochures, as to speed, technical wizardry, comfort and entertainment. The brochures waxed lyrically about the various ports of call, many providing considerable detail as to the historical and cultural attractions to be found; and, inevitably, much was made of the health-giving qualities of sea air and promenading the decks. The Royal Mail, extolling its spring cruises to the Mediterranean in 1927, after declaring that on its route 'the globe is sunniest and the sea its bluest', reached near literary heights –

There are lands where 'Spring' is not just a name of fragrant memory. Why should you be cheated of that delicious season

Royal Mail Line poster, design by Freda Beard, c.1920.

Above: 'Orient Cruises Norway' poster, design by Bernard Venables, 1933.

Left: Brochure cover for 'P&O Summer Cruises' to Norway, 1913.

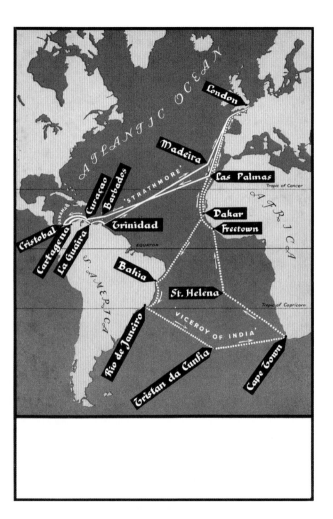

year after year because you live in the North? Resignation is a virtue – sometimes – but let it serve you on some other occasion; decide now to pursue SPRING even though it be into three continents. For they do know the season in the South; all around the Mediterranean shores and out into the Canaries and lovely Madeira they have their unfailing return of the blossoms, and sweet ethereal odours, and light, warm breezes – and of the new green on everything that grows.

That they were equipped technically with the most up-to-date equipment was ever a feature of the brochures, sometimes blinding the reader with science –

...propelled by turbo-electric machinery [the latest system of marine propulsion] and has mechanical ventilation throughout.

The development of facilities and interior design aboard cruise ships ran roughly parallel to what was going on ashore. Advertisements assured potential cruisers that everything was as up-to-date as could be, early advertisements and brochures making much of the use of electricity, refrigeration, wireless, and so on. The Royal Mail's Arcadia in 1927 detailed, in its brochure, that it was 'fitted with Wireless, Telegraphy, and Submarine Signalling', and that all cabins contained 'electric fans, lights and bells'. In the mid-30s the Orient line was bragging of being the first cruisers to have fire alarms and air conditioning. Baths and toilet facilities were shared well into the 1930s. The Royal Mail advertisements declared 'hot and cold running water in all the cabins' but made no mention of baths; and as late as 1938 Cunard's 'Franconia' still had some cabins without baths and some without toilets.

Opposite page: Front and back cover for a P&O Winter Cruises brochure, design by Norman Wilkinson, 1939.

And when it came to décor, many cruisers clung on to the historic and manorial style, some up to the onset of WWII. A description of the 'Asturia', included –

> The first-class smoke room was decorated in the manner of William and Mary, whilst the dining room was in the style of Christopher Wren.

Furness Withey's 'The Monarch of Bermuda', cruising in the 1930s, had décor described as 'a mixture of Art Deco and gentlemen's club'. Even when swimming pools came aboard they were given the historic treatment as for example those in Canadian Pacific's 'Empress of Australia' that were described as 'Pompeian'. It took the likes of architects, such as Brian O'Rorke for the Orient Line in the 1930s, and Sir Hugh Casson, in the 1960s, with the Canberra, to design ships used for cruising to introduce functional modernism, exposing passengers to the elements and to what was going on outside the vessel, rather than cocooning them in historic splendour inside.

When it came to entertainment, the early cruises offered deck games such as quoits, potato races, tug-of-war and thread needle races, with indoor sedentary pursuits as chess, and the card games whist, euchre and cribbage; and then there would be dancing and very frequently fancy dress. Gambling would take place daily on a number of possibilities, most often as to the punctuality of the ship's run. Much of these early amusements would be run by the crew who would make use of what talents lay amongst them as a note of one Chief Engineer rendering 'Two Eyes of Blue' in an impromptu concert. In the 1930s exercise and sunbathing took over as the major occupation during the day, cruisers by now having sundecks and swimming pools, and even a tennis court, as on Canadian Pacific's 'Empress of

Opposite page, left: Poster for P&O Cruises, design by D. Bailey, 1939.

Opposite page, right: Poster for P&O, design by Gilroy, 1935.

Orient Line
R.M.S. ORONSAY

Britain'. P&O's brochure for its cruises on the Viceroy of India and the Strathmore listed how passengers might be kept busy –

> …meeting new people, joining in happy little parties on runs ashore, cheery sports and games and dances, swimming and sunbathing – and all under blue skies and over smooth blue seas, sunshine by day, moon and starlight by night.

Brochures, sometimes subtly, sometimes more obviously, set out to embrace all possible passenger needs – whether to be on the go and busy or leisurely and relaxed, whether to be sociable or do one's own thing. Typical was the Orient Line offering cruises to the Mediterranean, Adriatic, Canary Islands and Madeira in 1933 –

You do not like crowds and you imagine that you will not be able to get away from your fellow passengers. In 'Orford', 'Orantes' and 'Orama' you will have plenty of room to have as much or as little company as you please, to be as lazy or as strenuous as you like. You cannot be too old, too middle-aged or too young for a Cruise, and that is why so many families find it an ideal form of holiday. Everyone can enjoy himself in his own way.

Organising excursions ashore, in the early years of cruising, was often the responsibility of the passengers themselves, but soon companies began to have an official on board to arrange things. Sometimes the shipping lines would have links to the Thomas Cook's office at the point of call, if there was one, and made use of its established land tours. These excursions could just be for part of a day, or, on more luxurious cruises, could extend to as much as a week. A Cunard World Cruise, in 1938 offered a two-day tour of Bali – 'to centres of typical Balinese native life. Balinese music and dance performance with a tour of the island'; or a week's tour of Bombay

Opposite page: Menu from 1958 for R.M.S. Oronsay of the Orient Line, complete with logo design by Edward McKnight Kauffer.

Right and far right: Two studies for posters created for the Orient Line by Harry Hudson Rodmell, undated.

with train journeys to Delhi and to Agra to see the Taj Mahal, or a two-day tour of California with drives around Los Angeles and visits to Beverley Hills, Hollywood and the Beaches.

The post-war years brought mixed fortunes to the cruising industry. In the immediate post-war period P&O and the Orient Line became engrossed with runs for emigrants to Australia. These were years of austerity when people could not afford cruises, certainly not lengthy ones. There was, however, a period of currency control, when people realized their sterling cash allowances would indeed go further

ORIENT LINE CRUISES 1936

ORIENT LINE CRUISES

MEDITERRANEAN · ADRIATIC
CANARY ISLANDS · MADEIRA

cruising on a British registered ship, just being used for trips ashore; but when deregulation of allowances came the cruising market sagged.

By the 1960s, with air travel on the increase, most shipping lines were converting their fleets, normally on regular routes, to cruising; and by the 70s some lines, as the Royal Mail, Union Castle and Shaw Saville were actually bowing out of the cruising market altogether, focusing on freight rather than passengers. By this time cruising from British ports was largely in the hands of Cunard and P&O with such icons as the Canberra, the Oriana and Queen Elizabeth II. It was not until the 1970s that P&O bought the American Princess Line, and not really until the 1990s that cruising regained its pre-war popularity. Eventually an entente grew up between the shipping and aviation companies and flights began to feed cruises, each scratching the other's back.

Of all aspects of holidaying, apart from travelling by rail, the publicity and advertising for cruising stands clear in the quality of its design and illustration. As LNER was a leader in railway publicity, with Southern Railway a runner-up, so the Royal Mail Line and the Orient Line probably can be said to have led the field for the design of cruising advertising, with P&O and Cunard on their tails. Although much use was made of the work of 'fine' artists in the early years, with the mere adding of the appropriate tags to an artist's oil or water colour painting, the shipping companies increasingly commissioned commercial artists and designers who had a better understanding of marketing and knew how to catch people's eyes. A few later exceptions were the Orient Line's use of Norman Wilkinson, and Blue Funnel's commissioning of Kenneth Shoesmith, both well-known marine artists.

In the 1920s the advertising and publicity for the Royal Mail Line was continuously receiving commendation in the design press, as

Opposite page, left: Brochure cover for Orient Line, design by Richard Beck, 1936.

Opposite page, right: Brochure for Orient Line Cruises, design by Norman Wilkinson, 1933.

Royal Mail Line advertisement, as featured in *Vogue*, January 1961.

it was using some of the most popular commercial artists of the time – 'Shep' of the Baynard Press, Aldo Cosomati, Austin Cooper, Frank Newbould and Fred Taylor, with the rare inclusion of a woman artist, Freda Beard. Taylor, Newbould and Cooper belonged to LNER's 'select 5', artists on subsidies from the company on condition they did not work for competitors of the railway industry; shipping companies, also competitors when it came to holidaying, seem to have been discounted in the deal.

The Royal Mail Line sent Fred Taylor on one of its ships to South America, as P&O had given Thackeray a free berth hoping to get a good write-up but in this case to derive some useful sketches. And that was what Taylor provided – sketches that were later used in the company's publicity and about which Bradshaw, the 1920's guru when it came to commercial art, commented on their novel attractiveness –

> ...the eye tired of coloured photographs of gloomy saloons and endless vistas of promenade decks.

The Orient Line's commissioned artists were equally impressive. Although initially it had made use of Wylie, a marine artist and Royal Academician, for illustrating the company's first tome like Guide, it tended, thereafter to turn to commercial artists, the next generation to those used by the Royal Mail, with the odd overlap, as Frank Newbould. It too had an artist – the renowned wood engraver Robert Gibbons – make drawings from a cruise, which were later used in a variety of ways, one making a remarkable front for the company's 'Records of a Cruise'. Other notable Orient Line artists in the 1920s were Horace Taylor and C.F. Tunniclife, better known for his studies of birds and animals.

Poster for Orient Line Cruises, design by James de Holden Stone, c.1950.

Dorrit Dekk advertisement for the Orient Line, undated.

Dorrit Dekk advertisement for the Orient Line, undated.

ORIENT LINE

Agents :
THOS. COOK & SON LTD.

CRUISES 1937

In the 1930s the Orient Line commissioned work from artists at the Reimann School Studio, lately established in London, and from one of the iconic graphic artists of the inter-war years, Edward McKnight Kauffer. His publicity work for the Line's 'Orion' and his design of the company's symbol, along with its posters, brochures and even luggage labels, brought modernism to shipping graphics. In the post-war years the Orient Line fished from yet another generation of artists, the New Zealander, John Bainbridge, the eccentric collagist Dorritt Dekk, and that generation's icon, Abram Games. Dorritt Dekk, who was to design many advertisements and posters, particularly for Air France, was a rarity, for along with being female, she brought humour to cruise advertising, which was so surprisingly lacking.

EPILOGUE

Curiously, apart from odd exceptions issuing from the railway companies and a few shipping lines, much of the publicity and advertising in relation to holidaying tended to be conservative, even hackneyed, when it came to graphic design; and few companies and agencies went out of their way to attract and make use of the major graphic artists. Generally, they were to steer clear of 'modernism' or, indeed, of any other movement or trend in art or typography.

The sky was always blue, the sea blue-green and the sand yellow; families were always smiling and seeming to really enjoy each other's company, joining in with each other's activities; where adults were portrayed the women were always slim, good-looking and fashionably dressed (but not outré), the men suitably muscular; and there might even be a slight hint of romance somewhere in the air.

Although holidaying is about having fun, the advertising of holidays rarely tapped into the humour, the English whimsy, that was used so effectively, in the period, to sell such products as petrol, tobacco and drinks. Seasides could have their saucy McGill postcards, but there humour remained, not infecting the plethora of leaflets, brochures, and advertisements enticing would-be holidaymakers to resorts and their entertainments.

For graphic design historians the field is something of a challenge, for relatively little of all this ephemera, where illustrated, carried the artist's name. When auction houses have their occasional sales of travel and holiday posters, 'anon.' is to be seen as frequently as a name. Yet advertisers and publicists obviously had some understanding of the pull of good graphics, for although the inner pages of their leaflets and brochures would be full of greyish photography, the covers would ofttimes be given over to the graphic illustrator and to colour.

Holidaying publicity and advertising is likely to prove a richer vein to mine for social scientists, who, with patience and a little imagination, could well discern trends in social norms and mores in the different decades covered by this book, comparing the pre- and post-war periods – the well-heeled giving way to the masses, home resorts to far-away destinations, the railway to the car and the plane, family holidays to individual generation choices. But to those like ourselves, collecting and pouring over the holiday ephemera of the time, we must admit that it has been just an indulgence in nostalgia, and, as with most ephemerists, a happy haven in times of turmoil.

BIBLIOGRAPHY

1925 Percy V. Bradshaw, *Art in Advertising*, The Press Art School.

1991 Piers Brendon, *Thomas Cook: 150 years of popular tourism*, Secker & Warburg.

2000 John K. Walton, *The British Seaside: Holidays and Resorts in the Twentieth Century*, Manchester University Press.

2000 Miriam Akhtar & Steve Humphries, *Some Like it Hot: The British on Holiday at home and abroad*, Virgin Publishing.

2004 Roger Cartwright & Clive Harvey, *Cruise Britannia*, The History Press.

2005 Jill Hamilton, *Thomas Cook: The Holiday-maker*, Sutton Publishing.

2005 Susan Barton, *Working-class Organisations and Popular Tourism 1840–1970*, Manchester University Press.

2005 Ian Yearsley, *A History of Southend*, Phillimore.

2007 Richard Paramor, *The Story of Victoria Coach Station*, Venture Publications.

2008 Nick Robins, *The Cruise Ship*, The History Press.

2009 Prof. Vanessa Toulmin, *Winter Gardens, Blackpool*, Boco Publishing Ltd.

2011 Prof. Vanessa Toulmin, *Blackpool Tower*, Boco Publishing Ltd.

2011 Prof. Vanessa Toulmin, *Blackpool Pleasure Beach*, Boco Publishing Ltd.

2011 Sylvia Endacott & Shirley Lewis, *Butlin's: 75 Years of Fun*, The History Press.

2012   Prof. Vanessa Toulmin, *Blackpool Illuminations*,
Boco Publishing Ltd.

2013   Alf Townsend, *The Charabanc*, Amberley.

2016   Kathryn Ferry, *The Nation's Host: Butlin's and the story of the British Seaside*, Viking.

For serious students of seaside history John K. Walton's wonderfully comprehensive tome is the essential textbook in spite of 200 or so pages in small font, with sentences of over 100 words, and paragraphs over a page in length, and not one illustration of a pier or sandcastle as light relief.

The majority of the images come from private collections of ephemera. Acknowledgements to Thos. Cook & Son for the small cartoons we borrowed from their vintage brochure 'Hints for your Holidays'.

Ruth Artmonsky

Stella Harpley

Ruth & Stella